PEACE FROM GOD'S WORD

COLORS: HOW DO YOU SAY IT?
(065) FOREIGN LANGUAGE

0688069487   DUNHAM, MEREDITH

DATE DUE

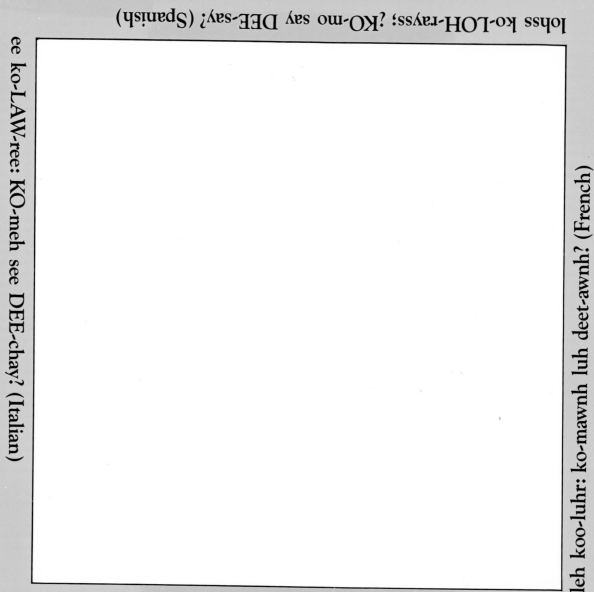

leh koo-luhr: ko-mawnh luh deet-awnh? (French)

lohss ko-LOH-rayss; ¿KO-mo say DEE-say? (Spanish)

ee ko-LAW-ree: KO-meh see DEE-chay? (Italian)

colors: how do you say it? (English)

Colors:

How Do You Say It?

English · French · Spanish · Italian

by Meredith Dunham

Lothrop, Lee & Shepard Books   New York

$9.25

First Edition   1   2   3   4   5   6   7   8   9   10

Library of Congress Cataloging in Publication Data
Dunham, Meredith.   Colors: how do you say it?
English, French, Italian, and Spanish. Summary: Illustrations of various objects in
different colors are accompanied by the appropriate descriptive words in English, French,
Spanish, and Italian. 1. Color—Juvenile literature. 2. Picture-books for children. [1. Color.
2. Picture dictionaries, Polyglot] I. Title.   QC495.5.D86   1987   535.6   86-27739
ISBN 0-688-06948-7   ISBN 0-688-06949-5 (lib. bdg.)

To my brother, Douglas James Dunham

oon ray-GAH-lo RO-ho (Spanish)

oon ray-GAH-lo ROHS-so (Italian)

unh kah-doh roozh (French)

a red present (English)

un regalo rosso

un regalo rojo

un cadeau rouge

a red present

ell KAY-ssoh ah-ma-REE-yo (Spanish)

eel fohr-MAH-ghee-oh JAHL-lo (Italian)

luh fro-mahzh zhohn (French)

yellow cheese (English)

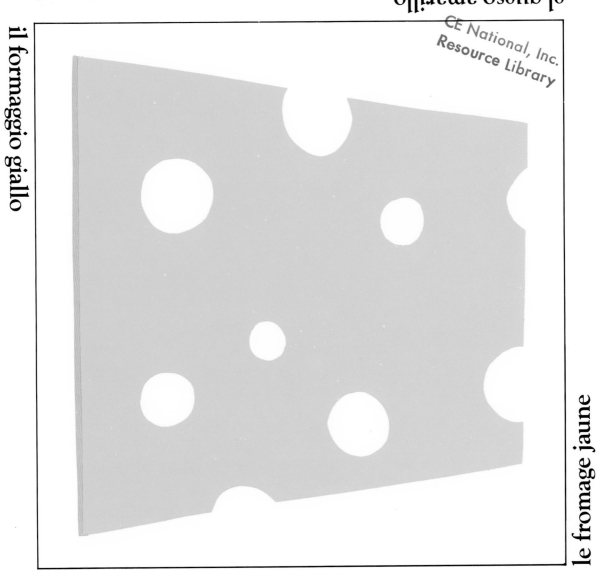

il formaggio giallo

le fromage jaune

yellow cheese

OON-ohss cho-ko-LAH-tayss moh-RAY-nohss (Spanish)

DEH-ee chyohk-ko-lah-TEE-nee mahr-RO-nee (Italian)

deh sho-ko-lah brunh (French)

brown chocolates (English)

brown chocolates

dei cioccolatini marroni

unos chocolates morenos

des chocolats bruns

OON-ahss FLOH-rayss ro-SSAH-dahss (Spanish)

DEH-ee fee-OHR-ee RAW-zah (Italian)

deh fluhr rohz (French)

pink flowers (English)

dei fiori rosa

unas flores rosadas

des fleurs roses

pink flowers

OON-ohss KOO-bohss mo-RAH-dohss (Spanish)

DEH-ee KOO-bee VYOH-lah (Italian)

deh kewb POORpruh (French)

purple blocks (English)

dei cubi viola

des cubes pourpres

purple blocks

oon tay-LAY-fo-no BLAHN-ko (Spanish)

oon tay-LAY-fo-noh BYAHN-ko (Italian)

unh teh-leh-fun blawnh (French)

a white telephone (English)

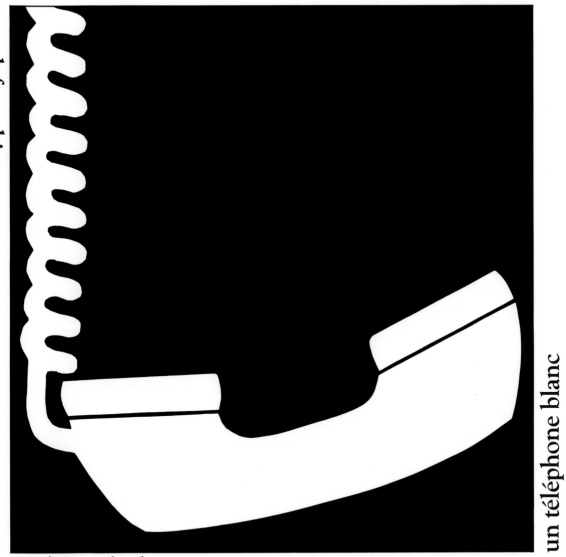

un telefono bianco

un téléphone blanc

a white telephone

OON-ah ess-kah-LAY-rah ah-SOOL (Spanish)

OON-ah SKAH-lah blu (Italian)

ewn eh-shell bluh (French)

a blue ladder (English)

una escalera azul

una scala blu

une échelle bleue

a blue ladder

green frogs (English)

DEHL-leh RAH-nay VAYR-dee (Italian)

OON-ahss RAH-nahss VAYR-dayss (Spanish)

deh greh-nwee vehrt (French)

delle rane verdi

unas ranas verdes

des grenouilles vertes

green frogs

OON-ah nah-RAHN-ha ah-nah-rahn-HA-dah (Spanish)

oon ah-RAHN-chyah ah-rahn-CHYOH-nay (Italian)

ewn oh-rahnzh oh-rahnzh (French)

an orange orange (English)

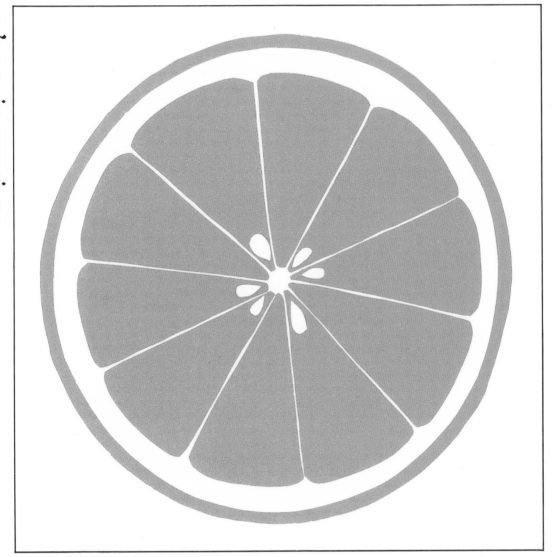

un'arancia arancione

una naranja anaranjada

une orange orange

an orange orange

oon TREH-no NAY-ro (Italian)

unh tranh nwahr (French)

a black train (English)

un treno nero

un tren negro

un train noir

a black train

A Note on How You Say It

Read the pronunciation guides as if you were reading English text, accenting the syllables in capital letters. This will give the approximate sound of the French, Spanish, and Italian phrases. It can only be approximate because each language has some sounds that do not exist in English.

In French, the R is pronounced far back in the throat. The U (represented here as EW) is pronounced by rounding the lips for OO and saying EE instead. The nasal sound represented as a vowel plus NH (like ANH) is made by saying the vowel "through the nose."

In Spanish, the R is trilled with the tip of the tongue. A double R (RR) is trilled longer than a single R.

In Italian, the R is also trilled. A double consonant is pronounced longer than a single consonant.

Many vowel sounds in English are actually combinations of sounds. For example, if you say the word *make* slowly, you will hear EH and EE in the sound of the *a*. In French, Spanish, and Italian, the vowels are pure—containing only one sound.

If you listen to a native or trained speaker of these languages, you will notice other differences. But that's no reason not to have the fun of saying it in French, Spanish, and Italian!